To Jimmy, best wishes
Christine De Luca.

VOICES
&
SOUNDS

CHRISTINE DE LUCA

Poems in English and Shetland dialect

THE SHETLAND LIBRARY

ISBN 0 904562 44 1

Published by Shetland Library, Lerwick, 1995.

Printed by Shetland Litho, Lerwick, Shetland.

for

da young fok o Shetland
to help keep you in your midder-tongue

Shö gae her skalds da pooer ta spaek wi wirds o might;
An noo dey staand aroond her, sae nane ta her can licht.
Da sangs at we sing an da stories at we tell,
Dey're link - stens apon her röf ta hadd him fae da gael.

from 'Wir Midder-Tung' by VAGALAND
after the Danish of LEMBCKE

ACKNOWLEDGEMENTS

Some of these poems have appeared in the following journals: Chapman, Lines Review, Scots Glasnost, Spectrum, The New Shetlander; and in The School of Poets Calendar and The Big Green Yonkly Anthology. A selection of the dialect poems have also been broadcast on BBC Radio Shetland.

The author would like to thank the following people and organisations:

the Library for contributing financially, and in particular, John Hunter, Chief Librarian, for his support;

the Shetland Arts Trust for grant aid towards publication;

Olive Gibson for typing the manuscript;

John Graham, Editor, The New Shetlander, for encouragement over the years;

Kenneth Rae, Shetland Jewellery, for permission to copy two brooch patterns: the "Quendale Beast" (adapted by his father, Jack Rae) and the "Three Nornes" (designed by Jack Rae);

Cilla Robertson for her art work;

Pat Robertson for permission to quote from her husband's poem "Wir Midder Tung";

Tessa Ransford and members of the School of Poets, Edinburgh, for constructive criticism;

Alan Victor for his design work.

Contents

Foreword   *ix*

Glancing backwards

Viking landfall   *1*
Thule revisited   *2*
Wife in ston   *4*
Gyaain fur da mylk   *6*
Paet wark   *8*
Gyaain ta da eela   *10*
Some fling   *12*
Private laand   *14*

Change

City life   *17*
Edinburgh volte-face   *18*
Spring break   *19*
Island home-comings   *20*
Lönabrack at Littlure   *21*
Respite in Wonderland   *22*
Middle age comes kindly   *24*

Relationships

Queer things, smiles   *27*
Body chemistry   *28*
Moment of belonging   *29*
Tagidderness   *30*
Approaching Christmas   *31*
Breaking the journey   *32*
Dee an me   *33*
Love can be   *34*
Surface tension   *35*
A baby's smile   *36*
Brekken beach, nort Yell   *37*
On the death of my mother at midsummer   *38*
On the death of my father at Christmas   *39*

A *peerie codicil (dialect and English versions)*   41
Brooch with three Nornes   42
In your orbit   43
Fowl play   44
Dominion   45
Alzheimers   46
South African poet   48

Journey

Airborne over Orkney   51
Tirricks   52
Wan wirld at Bluemull Soond   53
Focal length   54
Life falls in pleasant places   55
Voices of Quendale Bay (dialect and English versions)   56

Foreword

The Shetland Library has established a reputation for publishing work of quality, two examples of which are Donaldson's "Courtbook of Shetland..." and "MacDiarmid in Shetland". This, however, is the first publication in the field of imaginative or creative writing. The quality of this collection of poems will act as a benchmark for future publications.

It has been a privilege to have been given the opportunity to publish Christine de Luca's first collection and it has been a pleasure to work with the poet herself. I know you will derive equal pleasure from reading her work.

J. G. Hunter A.L.A.
Chief Librarian

GLANCING
BACKWARDS

A pride o langboats
wast fae Bergen
wi dreams o land
an lipperin kyists o mel;
spirits lift is Shetland rises
low apo da prow, an Viking een skile
shores fur meids, telt o
bi winter fires.

Ta starb'rd
da bicht o Uyeasoond
whar Thor rived Fetlar
wi his tirn nev, an balled her
clean soothbye;

dan roond bi Hascosay
ta peerie Aywick
an deeper Otterswick;
an on ta Gossabrough:
a gentle daal, wi hoop o sand
an tang ta sweeten soorest aert;
a burn fur water an a mill
an space ta bigg an dell.

Der sails wir lowered, oars aesed,
boats couped owre fur kye ta platsh ashore
an aa da proil o conquest
o mankind owre aert
wis lowsed apo da sand.

Dey'd mak der mark at Gossabrough.
In Norrawa, der saga wid be rösed
roond idder fires.

---

lipperin: *overflowing*; mel: *(oat)meal*; skile: *peer*; meids: *landmarks for boats*; rived: *tore*;
Fetlar: *an island*; tirn: *angry*; nev: *fist*; balled: *threw*; dan: *then*; peerie: *little*; daal: *dale*;
tang: *seaweed*; aert: *earth*; bigg: *build*; dell: *dig*; der: *their*; couped: *capsized*; platsh:
wet, heavy walking; proil: *belongings, booty*; lowsed: *poured*; Norrawa: *Norway*; rösed:
praised; idder: *other*.

In late simmer dey cam: we'd hear
der muffled throb: Norske boats
makkin fur laand.

An dan we'd see dem, far oot bi Linga,
plooin da voe wi a frush o froad
an maas divin.

Tae men dat fished da Foula shaalds, a voe
an hooses strung alang da banks
wis maistlins hame.

We'd sprit tae beat dem tae da pier, watch
is dey aeged in peerie wyes, wan bi wan
muvin ta rest.

Der boats wir gowld an white, neebin
lik dunters i da jap, nay sicht o varg,
aathin tuckit in an trig.

A line o bairns, we'd luk, an dey wid smile:
dey hed da very cast o wir faiders,
uncles, bridders.

We couldna spaek tae dem, but liftit
wirds wrocht fae common treeds: we'd rin hom
wi a skurtfoo o soonds.

We'd wave is dey daandered tae da shop, skoit
is dey stunkit back wi a hail o sweeties
fur der bairns.

Dey'd cum alang aboot da nicht
wi a piece o shark: mam wid spread da maet,
faider a map.

He'd shaw dem names der forebears hed gien
ta every gyo, every broo an croft, lik Brunnatwatt
an Leravoe.

An dey'd see kent names lik Kurkigarth an Grönivoe
Trölligarth, Stapness, Pointataing, Stove
an Dale.

An we wid watch an winder if da bairns o lang ago
wid a rin ta hoid, whin dey sa da soondless Norskes
i da voe.

Norske: *Norwegian*; dan: *then*; dem: *them*; frush: *spurt*; froad: *froth, surf*; maas: *seagulls*;
shaalds: *shallows*; voe; *sea loch*; maistlins: *almost*; sprit: *dash*; peerie wyes: *cautiously*;
neebin: *dozing*; dunters: *eider ducks*; jap: *choppy waves*; varg: *messy work*; aathin:
everything; trig: *tidy*; cast: *resemblance*; wrocht; *worked, made*; treeds: *threads*; skurtfoo:
armful; daandered: *sauntered*; skoit: *peer*; stunkit: *panted*; hail: *a catch (of fish)*; aboot
da nicht: *during the evening*; maet: *food*; gyo: *deep, narrow sea inlet*; broo: *brow*; hoid:
hide; sa: *saw*.

3

(An imaginative reconstruction of the Gloup disaster, 1881, when 58 fishermen drowned in a storm)

On a knowe at Gloup
dere's a wife in ston
glinderin.

A scry o sixerns
med fur da far haaf,
lug sails dippin, wind risin.
I da mirknen, a mön-broch;
i da mornin a barmin sea.
Bi da heicht o da day
seeven mile o heuks spent;
da tap o Rönas cam an gud
trow lumps o sea.

Whedder ta haul
or cut an run,
loss twa ton o cod, an risk
a gowsterit laird?

Some turned for hom
while licht held;
some demmelled on,
hauling
kavvellin;
waves brook owre dem
dey höved dem back.

Tows wir cut:
waas o water smored dem
brucks o boats,
last gaspin handhads
slockit.

Dat day
ten boats gud doon:
six fae Gloup
an een fae Fethaland
fae Haraldswick
fae Rönas Voe
an Havera.

On every broo
lippenen een skiled seawirds
wadder empty.

On a knowe at Gloup
dere's a wife in ston
glinderin.

---

glinderin: *peering, eyes half closed*; scry: *à host, swarm*; sixerns: *six-oared fishing boats*; med: *made*; da: *the*; haaf: *deep sea fishing grounds*; mirknen: *twilight*; mön-broch: *circle of light round the moon*; barmin: *seething*; heuks: *hooks*; Rönas: *name of highest hill in Shetland*; gud: *went*; gowsterit: *overbearing*; demmelled: *pitched, taking in water*; kavvellin: *removing hooks*; höved: *threw*; tows: *long fishing lines*; waas: *walls*; smored: *smothered*; brucks: *remnants*; slockit: *extinguished*; broo: *brow of hill*; lippenen: *expectant*; een: *eyes*; skiled: *peered*.

Da shortest gaet ta Bardister
wis up da daal, makkin a trenkie
trowe unma 'an girse,
roond bi da lochside
an toons o Kurkigert;
on bi da paety hols
atween da lochs - but no owre near
fur fok said you wid laand "doon under"
if you weet your feet -
owre Vatnabrug, a muckle slab
across da burn, smoothed
trowe centuries
bi trows an traivellers.
Hit wis wir Rubicon in simmer:
nae shunner crossed
dan tirrick squadrons scrambled
ta warn wis aff der nests.
We'd rin, pel flailin owre wir heads
ta hadd dem aff,
spangin stanks o yallow blugga
shasted bi da caald clos pirr o wings.
At last, da nae man's laand o Bardister,
an der retreat. Warm whalps
wid rin ta meet wis:
a thoosand licks, an aa wir fear
o hameward baff
wis gien.

Anidder simmer gaet wis owre da hill;
anidder wirld: wild open heogan,
moss an hedder-kowes,
berries, sookies, drummie-bees
 - sookies gae'd a snyirk
when pooed, an cam clean oot;
wan flooer, wan honeyed sook,
primeval gadderin -

Whaaps an peewits keepit watch;
dey nivver muv'd but passed
der warnin cries aroond.
Nests wir denkies i da grund
wi eggs or bruckit shalls.

At last, leg-weary, we'd cum apo
da hill-grind, twa hooses
an da riggs o Bardister.

Pels lined da porch,
some wi blaand or bleddick
sharp-smelled an snipperin;
fur wis, fresh mylk
still warm.

We'd mak fur hom, pel daddin,
unawar o fu a kirn o memory
wid turn sae lang
an still sustain.

---

gaet: *path*; daal: *valley*; trenkie: *narrow passage*; trowe: *through*; unma 'an: *unmown*; girse: *grass*; toons: *arable strips*; paety hols: *peaty hollows*; trows: *trolls*; shunner: *sooner*; tirrick: *arctic tern*; pel: *milk-pail*; hadd: *hold*; spangin: *leaping*; stank: *ditch*; blugga: *marsh marigold*; shasted: *chased*; pirr: *wind*; baff: *struggle*; heogan: *common hill pasture*; hedder-kowes: *bushy heather*; sookies: *lousewort (pink flower)*; drummie-bees: *bumble bees*; sniyrk: *squeak*; whaaps: *curlew*; denkies: *shallow hollows*; bruckit: *broken*; hill-grind: *hillgate*; riggs: *fields*; blaand: *whey*; bleddick: *buttermilk*; snipperin: *puckering*; daddin: *bumping*; kirn: *churn*.

7

Voar wark dune, tochts turned ta da hill,
tae a hairst o winter paets ta cut an cure:
faider'd set oot wi tushkar an wi spade
ta rip an flae an cast a bank or twa.
Dellin doon, liftin fae da soolp,
tushkar fleein, paets wheefed up an owre;
ootburg spreadin, dark daek risin:
rings o movement an even lines o aert:
a dance, a vynd wrocht oot
in space an time
sin fire first lowed.

Licht lentenin days, sun high apo wir backs,
we'd burst apo da hill
liftin da larks;
raise da mossy paets laid oot apo da broo,
dan set apo da daek, blue brittle brack.
Banks raised, we'd loup clean owre
-peerie legs aye langer, jumpin farder-
spang owre skyumpies
platsh da greesy greff.

As simmer opened oot, da aert cam dry
an greffs wir raised. We'd roog
an turn da half-dry paets, but aye fin time atween
ta tirl an headicraa, curse motts an mudjicks,
seek berries, shaste mooratoogs,
purl i da paety loch
an swittle taes.

Ta tak paets hame, a hidmost wrastle at da hill:
we'd rummel roogs, bag, borrow, fill kishies high
rinnin wi dem, kyempin, ta da rod;
hark an hear da tractor a dizzen times afore he cam
-aye late, a day's wark dune, a dizzen mödoos maa'd-
an whit a styooch o hentin, firin,
ballin bags on tap, maakin da lod.

As mirknen creepit in
we'd clim on tap
an ride da cuggly lod
lik monarchs.

Hame wi da hirdin, black paets
sookit herd an dry: a glöd
o winter warmth fae simmer's haand:
a varg, a strug, a spree:
a smile o simmer aert an sun an wind rowed up
ta hap da caald.

---

voar: *spring*; hairst: *harvest*; paets: *peats*; tushkar: *peat-cutting spade*; rip an flae: *prepare peat bank*; cast: *dig out peats*; dellin: *digging*; soolp: *soggy earth*; wheef: *swift movement*; ootburg: *outlay of peats*; daek: *wall of new cut peats*; vynd: *skill*; wrocht: *worked*; lowed: *blazed*; raise: *to set peats up in small pyramids to dry*; broo: *brow of hill*; loup: *jump*; peerie: *small*; spang: *bound*; skyumpies: *discarded mossy peat*; platsh: *wet, heavy walk*; greff: *bottom of peat bank*; roog: *gather in heaps*; tirl: *turn over, falling*; headicraa: *somersault*; mudjicks: *midges*; shaste: *chase*; mooratoogs: *ants*; purl: *poke investigatively*; swittle: *splash gently*; hidmost: *final*; wrastle: *struggle*; rummel: *collapse*; kishies: *cane baskets carried on back*; kyempin: *competing*; mödos: *meadows*; maa'd: *mown*; styooch: *dust rising*; hentin: *gathering*; firin, ballin: *throwing*; lod: *load*; mirknen: *twilight*; cuggly: *unbalanced*; hirdin: *from verb "hird", to harvest*; glöd: *glow*; varg: *dirty work*; strug: *toil*; spree: *fun*; rowed up: *wrapped up*; hap: *enfold, wrap warmly*.

9

(Going evening fishing for saithe)

Vaila darkenin fae aest ta wast,
wind faa'n awa;
eela nichts i da simmer dim.

Abune da tide, lik a sel, wir boat wid lie;
we hed ta tize her doon,
bulderin an traan owre da ebb
but nyiff i da sea.

Rowin oot bi wir kent wirld
ta da uncan moo o da Wastern Soond,
holms lay black on a sea an sky o gowld.

We'd row til da holm o Burrastow cam clos
dan drap da dorro;
een o wis wid aandoo, boos ta da wind.

Waands owre da starn,
piltocks nyggin:
up dey'd come wi a bummel,
sheenin, spricklin,
dan prammed an pechin at wir fit.

Lines unreffelled
owre da side again
roond an roond da skerry
waatchin fur froad braakin on da baas.
Gleg een, quick haands;
piltocks taakin
bucket fillin
ee mair time
maybe twa.
Dan aathin quiet an da hömin closin in.

Packin up wir proil, we'd mak fur hom,
blyde o kent lichts. We'd row
peerie wyes, owsin as we gud.
Abune wis, tirricks flitin
an a mird o maas laavin an divin,
plötin fur muggies.

We'd tak da boat in on a flowin tide,
dicht an shoard her, dan rin hom prood
i da darkenin wi a fraacht o fish.
We'd aet wir supper
tae tales o uncan Odysseys
in idder voes.

---

faa'n awa: *abating*; eela: *evening fishing for saithe*; simmer dim: *twilight*; sel: *seal*; tize:
entreat, tempt; bulderin: *clumsy*; traan: *perverse*; ebb: *foreshore*; nyiff: *nimble*; uncan:
unfamiliar; moo: *mouth*; holms: *rocky islands*; dorro: *handline*; aandoo: *row slowly*; boos:
bow; waands: *rods*; piltocks: *saithe*; nyggin: *tugging*; bummel: *floundering*; spricklin:
wriggling; prammed: *squeezed together*; unreffelled: *untangled*; froad: *froth*; baas:
submarine rocks; gleg: *alert*; aathin: *everything*; hömin: *twilight*; proil: *booty*; blyde: *glad*;
peerie wyes: *gently*; owsin: *baling water*; gud: *went*; tirricks: *arctic tern*; flitin: *scolding*;
mird: *throng*; maas: *seagulls*; laavin: *hovering*; plötin: *whining, begging*; muggies: *fish
guts*; flowin tide: *high tide*; dicht: *clean, tidy*; shoard: *prop*; fraacht: *load, burden*; idder:
other.

11

Some fling it was
practising for the school dance,
near the end of term
in the canteen shed:
a gym period wedged
between lunch and French.

Boys arrive, conscripts
with no appetite
for dancing; protect
vulnerable parts
with feigned indifference.

The flag goes up
a reel announced
boys are goaded,
push each other,
braced for contact.
Girls fret
they'll be left:
edge forward,
capitulate.

The sets are made:
territory claimed.
Palms sweat, arms crunch
in sockets.
Round for 8, back for 8
"wrong way, class 2"
and the squeak
of gym shoes braking
on linoleum.

"And now in 2's,
move up your set,
poussette!

A...way from the centre
turn, right or left
turn. Into the centre
turn right round
fall back
fall back."

There was bravery
and bruising
before the bell would ring.
Some fling.

Faces fornenst windows we stimed,
cuppit haands blockin oot da licht.
Ony a coose o bruck ta see.

On a knowe ahint da Haa
a skorie croogit in a röfless to'er;
wis hit whar ladies sippit tae
or whar da laird wid set his gless
apo sixerns in truck ta him
ta ken whar dey wid laand
der catch?

Dey'r aa gien noo:
a wye a life turned headicraa
vod is der haa.

I da kirkyerd
fenced aff fae aabody
der's a röd o wirds
apon a muckle stane;
an nettles cled
der hidmost privacy.

---

fornenst: *against*; stimed: *peered closely*; coose: *heap*; bruck: *useless material, refuse*;
ahint: *behind*; Haa: *laird's hall*; skorie: *young seagull*; croogit: *crouched*; hit: *it*; tae: *tea*;
gless: *telescope*; apo: *on*; sixerns: *six-oared fishing boats*; in truck: *servitude (payment in
goods)*; dey'r: *they've*; gien: *gone*; headicraa: *head-over-heels*; vod: *unoccupied*; is: *as*;
röd: *meaningless ramble*; cled: *clothe*; hidmost: *last, final*.

CHANGE

We are shelf-dwellers,
stacked up: people
insulated horizontally
and vertically
by bells and burglar alarms.

Our homes
have pain and partying
adjacent
and simultaneous.

Our moving
is metered out
by traffic lights:
staccato gods.

We make and spend:
our transactions
increasingly anonymous.

We are at the mercy
of each other: each sells
his separate skill.

We are slow to evolve
detachment;
to acquire the new survival skills.
Like ants, we retain
our communal gene
against adversity.

City of seven hills
rivalling Rome: you are
the big sister of all cities,
forever tut-tutting.

City of venerable skylines;
each morning you un-do yourself
like someone more anxious to save the wrapping
than enjoy the gift.

City of open spaces: for you
no strollers in the forum; merely
a scurry of solicitors, vellum-faced
with long north-facing days,
and little women, worn
from cleaning other people's stairs.

City of the great estates;
you have no outer wall, but numerous apartheids
charitably maintained.

City of seven hills
rivalling Rome: I hold your negative
to the light, and see
your true topography.

It is the nihilism I like
the almost lack of calendar
the near amnesia
of who and what I am;

no phone, no bearers
of busy tidings, good or bad;
everything on 'hold'

and in a room of no decisions
finding at last the slack tide
of sleep, in linen I shall not wash,

lying through depths of re-dreamed dreams
but no matter, dozing again, content
to judge time only by daylight
through thick curtains
gradual, sensing

a life-line spun out, pulled
through turbulence, now reeled in
slowly to renewal.

I remember the 'exiles':
they came north with the sun.
You could pick them out easily
by their impressiveness:
birds of passage, with distinctive plumage
and a new note in their throats.

Their spouses lingered
on the edges of conversations;
their children spoke in tutored tongues
and played cricket relentlessly
across bogs.

Now I have a city child
I bring him north.
He is the one apart,
with awkward smiles.

Laevin Burrastow, hills winter ochre
we lean inta da wind, alang banks' gaets.
Luckit bi da updraa, maas lift
ta plane in silence.

Drappin doon ta da loch o Quinnigyo
April sun is warm.
A pair o rain geese mak fur da hill
an a laverock is a ringin string
ta da lunder o ocean bass.

Climbin, we mak da bicht o Littlure;
Foula stepped apo da skyline.
Atlantic rollers brack,
kirn ita gyos,
höv spindrift;
black headlands settle
in a böl o froad,
sharpenin clooers.

Back o'er ta Quinnigyo, we crug
lik kittiwakes anunder banks, watch
bowes an corks drift seawirds.
Waves at's birled fae Labrador lirk in;
steer a sheeksin atween shalls an stons.

Doon owre da broo at last ta Burrastow,
wind-hattered but foo o newness.
Da sea kwilks in an oot,
a selkie basks,
an, fur a blink,
he taks wis back
ta wir beginnings.

---

lönabrack: *surf*; luckit: *tempted*; maas: *seagulls*; rain geese: *red-throated divers*; ringin string: *traditional Shetland fiddling involves the playing of two strings simultaneously, creating a resonance*; höv: *heave*; spindrift: *sea spray*; böl: *where an animal lies*; clooers: *claws*; crug: *crouch*; lirk: *crease, wrinkle*; sheeksin: *blethering*; kwilks: *makes a swallowing sound*; selkie: *seal*.

So this is respite care:
behind locked doors
a coiled spring of a woman,
ever tightening with age?
It seems your body has not slowed
to match your mind:
while most are phased
by television screens
or nod off into teacups
you craze up boulevards of corridors:
chasing that white rabbit,
on and on, up and down
creating a maze

out of a straight line.
Now bending to check, running;
your frantic hands splayed
along walls, at knee-height;
with all propriety frayed
now kirtling your skirt,
wiping it down, erasing
flowers painted on it.
Bend and run, bend and run:
what is it that you seek?
A little door, low down? A key,
golden to unlock a world?
Medicine to shrink you
to knee high; to find that exit,
that lost reality? What is it
that propels this race:
makes things seem other than they are,

compels this busyness? A trace
of madness, or a button
labelled self-destruct?
You dip and spin past nurses, shun
their gentle counsel:

riddles they are:
riddles bouncing off the walls:
bounce and catch; match them
to the answers as they fall

into this geriatric wonderland
where everything is falling,
falling. There is no respite
from time's ravages.
It is a savage thing, a grief, to murder
time: a pool of tears might bring
a sweet relief.

Middle age comes kindly:
it sidles up, steals
behind mirrors.

It calms the rash imperatives
of youth; that constant swash
and backwash of relationships;
that erosiveness of conquest,
of gouging personal landscapes.

Ahead, the quiet creep
of slow ebb tides,
wrinkling back down;
sustaining intimacies
imperceptibly:
- a Japanese theatre
of smallest movements -
a little lapping
at ease with discontent
and doubt.

Middle age comes kindly
its edges rounded:
and its touch
is light.

RELATIONSHIPS

A baby's smile
is a hale boady affair:
a pooster o airms an legs
seekin ta plaese.

A bairn's smile
wirks on wis, kyöderin
til we gie in.

A blind man's smile
is nae less fur hits eelessness:
learned ithoot seein
foo a smile bracks.

Da smile o an uncan boady,
- a blate risk o a kennin
we geng da sam gaet -
bals just enoych caution
tae da wind.

Da smile o a loved wan
- dat peeriest glink i da een at says
mair is we dare tink true -
caa's owre an biggs
at een an da sam time;
hit maks a bassel o pairtin.

---

hale: *whole*; pooster: *vigour*; kyöderin: *showing fondness, ingratiatingly*; foo: *how*; da: *the*; uncan: *unfamiliar*; blate: *shy*; kennin: *knowing*; geng: *go*; gaet: *path*; bals: *throws*; enoych: *enough*; peeriest: *smallest*; glink: *gleam*; een: *eyes*; at: *that*; tink: *think*; caa's owre: *knocks down*; biggs: *builds*; een: *one*; hit: *it*; bassel: *struggle*.

Can I believe you are
no more than atoms reeling
in intimate bombardment?
(Even when you sleep, they dance.)
And that your molecules
bonded this way and that
just hold back chaos?
What random wobbling
to produce such subtlety!
What sub-atomic spaces!
What emptinesses
to create such stature!
Such galaxies of wonder
is a man!

A high sun slanting
its escape through canopies
of leaf and cloud
seeks out a skylight
to this glade of buttercups.
Bright sun-soaked petals
newly glazed, reflect
a buttery beam
on smiling chins.

Like us, the flowers span
but the briefest blink of time:
no grand design, just
generations linked
haphazardly:
seeds on the wind
and dusty layers
of unnoteworthy lives.

But in the other's eye
for just the briefest moment
of belonging, we too reflect
a smile, exquisitely.

Twa hill lambs
fae uncan erts,
- een black an halliget;
een moorit, mair perskeet -
ta'en fae da heogan
tae a park,inbye;
cringed an teddered:
morroless.

Little winder
sae clos yokit, een poos
fornenst da tidder.

Hit taks a while
at best, ta muv as wan,
at warst, ta thole; ta see
dere's naethin war as
closness, whin hit's
reffelled up an wippit
in a snöd.

---

tagidderness: *togetherness*; uncan: *unfamiliar*; erts: *directions, places*; een: *one*; halliget: *wild*; moorit: *brown*; perskeet: *prim*; heogan: *common hill pasture*; cringed: *joined to a single tedder (tether)*; morroless: *not matching pair*; yokit: *yoked*; poos: *pulls*; fornenst: *against*; da: *the*; tidder: *other*; muv: *move*; wan: *one*; war as: *worse than*; reffelled: *tangled*; wippit: *bound together*; snöd: *twist*.

Winter solstice:
darkest day;
cost of summer light
relentlessly extorted
through tilted orbit
round a sun star.

Human orbits
are incongruent:
fields of force which pull
in opposition,
tilting seasons.

Approaching Christmas
equilibrium pervades
in a child's short shadow
and in the mystery
of a star.

I bundle up my love
and all its gladnesses,
shouldering the great lightness
through strange and unfamiliar lands.
Only with you am I the gypsy:
glad to unpack it all, such as it is,
to let it spill in all its silly wonder,
its seeming worthlessness.

And you unwrap it
with your gentle unsurprise:
in your hands it's full of brightness,
and value
and strange freedom.

But I must pack it up again,
and hurry on towards no destination,
content to break the journey
briefly.

Lambs playin picky
pheasants rinnin
dunters risin
dee an me

Gutter platshin
drush drooklin
burn trivvelin
dee an me

Bare hills gaanin
distance lippenin
baith virmishin
dee an me

Time near bi gyaan
hainin apo hope
wan oot o twa
dee an me

Time fur saain
time fur hirdin
time fur winderin
dee an me

---

dee: *you (familiar form)*; picky: *tag*; dunters: *eider ducks*; gutter: *wet earth*; platshin: *heavy, wet walking*; drush: *heavy drizzle*; drooklin: *soaking*; trivvelin: *feeling its way*; gaanin: *gazing*; lippenin: *expecting*; virmishin: *longing*; near bi gyaan: *mean*; hainin: *using sparingly*; wan: *one*; saain: *sowing*; hirdin; *harvesting*.

Love can be simply
an affinity
without causation.

Love can be duty:
fatigued clockwork
relentlessly rewound.

Love can be obsession:
a mythology, a creation
out of control.

Love can be quiet company;
merely a glance,
a dance of the imagination.

Love can be conquest:
a cornering of affection,
a captive end in itself.

Love can be an ambivalence
of pain and pleasure:
a retreat into measured response.

Love can be
a smiling voice
and a crying heart.

Must we forever live
between rocks and hard places
with words eroding dryly?
Must our verbal terrain straddle
grumbling fault-lines,
discontinuities?

Must the view be barren plateaux;
rigg-tops broken only
by wind-stunted trees?
Are there no dales,
no widths of greens?

Chuck words across the chasms
if you must, I am prepared
for impact: but rather
that you trudged words with you;
left the marks of journey on them,
brought them, laid them down
in gentle deposition.

Peerie ting
wi dy sprootin an flailin,
du gaffs an smiles
wi dy hale boady:
du could tresh coarn
wi yon legs o dine
an der wappin.

Dy face is a flaachter
an dy smile bides
as a glöd o licht
fae a dippin sun.

Naethin at's göd
could dave dis spunk
or trottle dy sang.

---

peerie ting: *little one*; dy: *your (familiar form)*; sprootin: *drooling*; du: *you (familiar form)*;
gaffs: *laughs*; hale: *whole*; tresh: *thresh*; coarn: *oats*; dine: *yours (familiar form)*; der:
their; wappin: *vigorous movement*; flaachter: *fluttering*; bides: *remains*; glöd: *glow*; göd:
good; dave: *diminish*; dis: *this*; spunk: *spark*; trottle: *throttle*.

A mile aff we catch a glisk
o Brekken beach: webbed
atween headlands, a glansin arc
o ancient shalls
sun sillered.

Waves aff Arctic floes
bank in; dey shade fae cobalt
tae a glacial green; swall
an brack, rim on rim
o lipperin froad.

We rin owre dunes
crumplin smora,
fling aff wir shön
birze sand trowe taes
dell an bigg it;
shaste da doon draa
o da waves, loup
der hidmost gasps.

Abune wis, solan plane an plummet
an on da cliff, a tystie
triggit up in black and white
gawps at wir foally.

Da sun draps doon ahint his keep
an we man leave
an Eden aert
ta him.

---

nort: *north*; aff: *off*; glisk: *glimpse*; glansin: *sparkling*; shalls: *shells*; sillered: *silvered*;
dey: *they*; lipperin: *overflowing*; froad: *surf, froth*; rin: *run*; smora: *clover;* wir: *our*;
shön: *shoes*; birze: *squeeze*; trowe: *through*; taes: *toes*; dell: *dig*; bigg: *build*; shaste:
chase; doon draa: *backwash*; loup: *leap*; der: *their*; hidmost: *final*; abune: *above*; solan:
gannets; da: *the*; tystie: *black guillemot*; triggit: *dressed up*; foally: *folly*; ahint: *behind*;
man: *must*.

June in the north is a convocation
of life: a barely dipping sun,
a shower of birdsong
and a suddenness of flowers.

My mother's room is still. She turns her eyes
at the call of raingeese: out of decay
the blue bird-brightness of her gaze
holds summer's tincture.

Time's at a standstill now: for years
she's chased and bullied it, imposed upon it,
filled it to the brim.
But now the pendulum is set
to pause at every turn.

She turns her eyes again, following
the birds' flightpath. Momentarily
they lift her world beyond
its withering perimeter.

I sit prepared, yet unprepared:
it is momentous, this threat of separation;
alternately focusing
and then eliminating thought.
Unfinished conversations hover: words
have an all or nothingness
about them. We lapse into a silent vocabulary
of eye and hand,
a collusion of smiles.

I watch her breath flicker
ever more feebly,
until at last the moment comes
unhurried
unremarkable: one final sip of June
then quietness.
Suddenly the raingeese call
wildly as they pass,
but no eyes turn.

I

On Christmas Eve
I fill a child's stocking
then journey
-motherless myself-
to ease a father
towards death.

Everywhere is Christmas:
an ambivalence
of pleasantries,
of trees and tinsel.

Balanced between
generations, I look
neither forward nor back,
in case the see-saw tips
beyond enduring.

The plane flies north
through a sympathy of fog.
I block out
a landscape of faces:
a little boy waiting
and a father dying.

II

You are diminished, father,
yet dismiss
our mutuality of pain
with smiles.
Days are short
nights go on and on:
I travel with you
and soothe you
as a mother would
to fearless sleep.

III

The funeral day arrives
with thin sun, damp wind;
it is still December:
that no-man's land
between Christmas and New Year.

In church, eyes blur between coffin
and decorated tree; I lean myself
against the notes of old hymns.

IV

Hands of family and friends
lower you to silence; each one of us
a testament of your enabling.

It is too cold to linger; already
the edges of the wreaths are bruised.

V

And now, my son
I have come back
to your season
your excitement.

We hang a new calendar;
the balance of the year
has tipped
and light returns.

Dinna lay me wi uncan fok
ta lie a thoosand year
sabbin dagidder; da stane
heavy, marking oot a piece o laand
ithoot meanin.

Slock me whick an clean:
lat da ess birl whaar hit wil:
nae monimints. A'm in dee:
an du's mi mindin.

A LITTLE CODICIL

Do not lay me between strangers
to lie a thousand years
co-mingling; the stone
heavy, marking out a territory
without meaning.

Quench me clean and quick:
let the ash fly lightly
where it will: no stone,
no plaque. I am in you:
you are my memorial.

Three Nornes:
no virgin goddesses
but swans,
sculpt silver.

Urd
symbol of the Past
hangs her head:
she does not see
where love lay.

Verdandi
holds the Present
under outstretched wings.
She too looks down
accepting destiny.
Her wingtips intertwine
with Past and Future: she exists
where they touch.

Only Skuld
born of the Future
lifts her eyes: hope
is the lithe curve of her neck.
Wintering will pass:
she will fly
with the tilting earth.

Birling moon man,
you and earth rotate
in harmony; revolve
in measured orbits.

How come you never turn your back;
and always, when you're full,
that smiling bannock of a face?
What of your other side,
the hidden one? Is its brow furrowed,
its tear ducts dry?

And is it really you who turns the tides,
heaps water in unreasonable fathoms;
you, of the coy entrance,
the little slip of light, back lit,
maturing full frontal?

What if I, whose cycle matches yours,
were to suspend belief, abandon
all myth magic, wipe you
from every fairy tale?
Suppose I acknowledge you as dull
and dry and inhospitable; forgive
your lusciousness as mere reflection?

Such truth could blind.

He's a handsome bird, the ostrich
with a lot to flaunt: fine feathers
and a now protected tail.
His plumes have graced coquettes
and chorus lines; trimmed
hats and bodices;
sent frissons through audiences.

His legs, built with karate in mind
edge out his rivals; acceleration
is galvanic. His flightless wings
with white designer trim
seem to impress:
the mating dance, primeval, unrehearsed:

three times, three partners
a clutch of twenty eggs:
three simultaneous families reared as one.
He bides his time, then when he's done his bit
by his arithmetic
he's up and off, head high
fast as a car. The females cry

and put their heads together
in the sand, to cool off presumably
or plot to even up the score.
The young ones tend to learn no more
than sex, survival of the fit.
Sharp exits and stunning entrances:
that's the way it is, with ostriches.

Ya mo me, widow,

meaning "frost woman": beyond

sensuality.

Mi bo jin, widow,

meaning "not yet dead person":

all purpose denied.

Slip from your shadows;

annihilate dominion.

Shake off those grave clothes.

This poem refers to two Japanese words for "widow".

I

The day centre

It seems no time at all
since, at the day centre,
you were visitor:
good at names,
you humoured, bolstered;
left people much the better
of your coming.

But now it's you
who cannot tell the day from night,
which street, which door is yours.
Within this vast unlearning
you barely know the scope
of your confusion.

Walking in
momentarily you turn,
hand outstretched in greeting.
A nurse catches it,
leads you to a chair,
a cushioned line around
this hardest edge.

That's it.
You take your place.

II

Respite care

You look different today
despite the smile.
Is it the lack of tie
or the poor shave?

Bits of sentences collapse
between brain and mouth:
a computer file struck
by a virus. Gaps which dangle
between nouns are too big
for leaps of inference;
there is anxiety
in both words and pauses;
it is tempting to smooth
their edges with inconsequentials.
Having lost the past and future
it seems you are pure being;
that you have made each instant
your stillest dwelling.

Yet you can smile that smile forever you
to take us back, and lead us on:
that almost first great human bond,
that simplest of complexities
remains.

Intrepid explorer,
exile out of Africa:
chronicler of place,
you map your words
on to a landscape,
illuminating margins
with monkish diligence.

You peer at its fond places
like doctor or optician
searching the eye;
bearing in from all angles
to unseen spaces.

You dessicate
its history:
peel off its skin
re-possess its bones; placate
its molecules.

No botanical illustrator
could look in shorter focus,
no draughtsman lift his eye
to more vanishing points,
no artist try.

JOURNEY

Outstretched below
the isles of Orkney lie:
skins of ancient monsters
patterned wildly.
Long sinuous members, golden fringed,
sleep deeply, unstirring;
great nostrils, quiet now
lapping a tide.
Abrupt headlands: lurking claws
mindful of lost sea struggles.

The sea, lightly creased,
caressing her trophy,
sings of the vanquished.

The swallows of the north arrive
excitedly, contesting old haunts:
raucous celebration
of a safe arrival.
Sunny sounds in northern skies;
their cries reminiscent
of shrill barter
in tropical bazaars.

Year upon year
they power their way
from arctic to antarctic;
their route precise,
mapped out instinctively.
Within a short life-span
a moon distance flown.

Then just as suddenly, they're gone,
anticipating winter.
Their receding cries chill
into Autumn stillness.

Tirricks: *arctic tern*

Linga bracks da Bluemull Soond
smooth is a neesick.
Tirricks lift fae ferry furrows,
sweep backwirds in circles
skoitin fur sillocks: dey dive
an rise in perfect verticals.
Anidder ferry comes an still dey laav:
whit strug fur sic a peerie paek.

Alang da banks
a swaabie tips an penks
traepin fur maet.
Tief at he is, he shastes dem
til dey drap der catch.

He'll no fant
nor yet his kind
while peerie tirricks fish
da Bluemull Soond.

is: *as*; neesick: *porpoise*; tirricks: *arctic tern*; skoitin: *looking*; dey: *they*; anidder: *another*;
laav: *hover*; strug: *toil*; peerie: *small*; paek:_ *bite, small amount of food*; banks: *sea cliff*;
swaabie: *great black-backed gull*; tips: *walks jauntily*; penks: *titivates, shows off*; traepin:
nagging; maet: *food*; tief: *thief*; shastes: *chases*; dem: *them*; fant: *be famished*.

From the train, the view today
is monochrome. Rain rivets
sea and sky and land:
shades of grey reflect
the inner eye. I hesitate
to check my colour vision
against clothes of passengers.

My eye is drawn
to drops of water
on the window: they race
like frantic sperm
across the glass.
Only raindrops,
yet they pull the focus short;
shut out landscapes
beyond reason.

A day ago,
through the same window,
there were a thousand
bright vanishing points.

(In memoriam Pan Am Flight 103, December 1988)

Life falls in pleasant places:
five unwarned miles
above the green and sheepfold slopes
a fragile tether cut
in one long hellish trice of severing.

The Christmas lights have gone from Lockerbie,
frail in a fireball,
and neighbours' greetings
doused in an infernal uttering.

For Lockerbie
no gold or frankincense
but only myrrh,
and a Christmas star
exploding
and the ungivenness of gifts.

The muttering of the puffins

> You're accustomed
> to puffins:
> beaks full of eels
> you think us clowns.
> We make you laugh?
> Look us in the eye
> and see us weep.

The complaining of the ewes

> Since before Ninian
> our lambs have chewed
> salt seaweeds.
> The foreshore is sour
> Ugh! What an aftertaste
> is in our throats!

The moaning of the otters

> We twist and turn in the sea
> for fun, hunt
> sweet fish, bluster
> freedom round creels.
> The tide has turned.
> Besmirched now
> we lick poison.

The song of the sea

> Take no heed! Take no heed!
> I've danced and I've scolded
> drowned that stinking barrel.
> I shall feed you: comfort you
> with whitest surf.

Quendale Bay: the site of the Brear oil tanker disaster in Shetland in January 1993.

Da tröttel o da tammie nories

> You're weel wint
> wi tammie nories:
> nebs foo o eels
> you tink wis cloons.
> We mak you gaff?
> Luk wis i da een
> an see wis gowl.

Da nyaarm o da yowes

> Sin afore Ninian
> wir lambs ir shampsed
> saat tang an waar.
> Da ebb is shilpet.
> Gadge! Whitna waageng's
> i wir trots!

Da oobin o da dratsies

> Wi tirl i da sea
> fur fun, hunt
> sweet fish; skirl
> freedom roond creels.
> Da tide is turned.
> We'r elted noo
> an lick pooshin.

Da sang o da sea

> Never leet! Never leet!
> A'm danced an a'm flet,
> smored yon grötti-barrel.
> I sal maet you;
> cöllie aboot you
> wi whitest froad.